Rollin'

Pickup Trucks

by James Koons

CAPSTONE PRESS
MANKATO

C A P S T O N E P R E S S

818 North Willow Street • Mankato, MN 56001

Printed in the United States of America.

Library of Congress Cataloging-in Publication Data
Koons, James, 1970–
    Pickup trucks/James Koons.
    p. cm.
    Includes bibliographical references and index.
    Summary: Introduces the pickup truck, its history, special parts and features, function as a utility vehicle as well as for play, and its future
    ISBN 1-56065-372-8
    1. Trucks--History--Juvenile literature. [1. Trucks--History.]
I. Title.
TL230.15.K6623 1996
629.223--dc20

                                    95-49101
                                      CIP
                                       AC

Photo credits
Peter Ford: cover, 4-8, 12, 16-33, 37, 40, 43
Dennis Pernu: 10, 14, 15, 34, 38, 42

Table of Contents

Words in **boldface** type in the text are defined
in the Glossary in the back of this book.

Chapter 1

Pickups are Everywhere

There are all kinds of trucks for all kinds of jobs. If you watch a busy road, you will see many kinds of trucks. But most of all, you will see pickup trucks.

Pickups were the first trucks made for general use. Before pickups, the only trucks on the road were big work trucks.

Pickups were made because people wanted small trucks they could use to pick up small loads. Farmers could come to town to pick up supplies and carry them back. Since the trucks

Whether you live in the city or the country, you can see pickups every day.

were used to pick up small loads, people called them pickups.

Pickups are used in many ways. In the city, workers use pickups to carry tools and supplies. In the country, ranchers use pickups to haul feed and hay to their livestock. Park rangers use pickups to patrol campgrounds.

Pickups can be fun, too. They can go places a car cannot. They can go through mud and shallow water.

Some people build pickups big enough to crush cars. Other people buy old trucks nobody else wants. They fix up the old pickups. When they are done, the pickups look brand new.

Whether you live in the country or the city, you can see pickups every day, being used in many ways.

Pickups were made because people wanted small trucks they could use to pick up small loads.

Chapter 2
Before Pickups

Before gasoline engines were invented, heavy wagons were used to make deliveries. The wagons were made of wood. They were pulled by horses.

Then inventors powered the heavy wagons with gasoline engines. These were the first trucks. They were much larger than today's pickups. They were helpful, but they were not perfect.

The first small trucks were known as light-duty trucks. Later, they became known as pickups.

They were difficult to steer because they had long **boxes**. They had thin wooden wagon wheels that could not support much weight. They got stuck in the mud a lot.

The first trucks did not have **cabs**. If it was raining, the driver got wet. If it was cold outside, the driver got cold.

Still, trucks were faster than wagons pulled by horses. Drivers could make more deliveries in less time.

Utility Trucks

In the early 1900s, car makers began to build **utility trucks**. Like cars, utility trucks were made of steel, rather than wood. Utility trucks had rubber tires that were wider and stronger than wagon wheels.

Most utility trucks were flatbeds. Instead of a box, they had a flat platform behind the driver's seat.

The first pickups looked a lot like cars.

Chevrolet and Dodge were building pickups by 1918.

The Pickup is Born

Utility trucks were still very large, though. Many workers wanted smaller trucks. All they needed was enough room for their tools or other small loads.

So automobile makers designed smaller trucks. They were called **light-duty** trucks. Later, they became known as pickups.

By 1918, Chevrolet and Dodge were building pickups. In 1925, the Ford Motor Company also began building pickups.

Henry Ford and the Pickup

In the early 1900s, Henry Ford (1863-1947) invented the assembly line system for building cars. On the assembly line, workers had different jobs. Cars made their way down the line as the workers did their jobs and added parts to the car. By the end of the line, the car was finished. The Model T was the first car built on the line.

Ford Motor Company started building pickups in 1925.

Ford's assembly-line system was efficient. Thousands of cars could be built in a short time. Ford was able to sell the cars at a low price.

Ford's company had been making utility trucks since 1905. When his competitors began making pickups, Ford was not far behind.

The most familiar part of a pickup is the box.

In 1924, Ford bolted a small box on the back of one of his famous Model T's. The next year, he began to build pickups on his assembly line. Ford pickups are still among the most popular in the world.

Chapter 3
Parts of a Pickup

The first pickups looked a lot like cars. Today, it is easy to see how a pickup is different from a car.

The Box

The most familiar part of a pickup is its box. Unlike flatbed utility trucks, the pickup box has walls. The walls keep **cargo** from blowing away or falling out of the box. Pickups come with either long or short boxes.

The first pickup boxes were called **stepsides**. They had a small step in front of

The Ford Motor Company began making boxes entirely out of steel in 1957.

each rear wheel. Until the 1950s, all boxes were stepsides. The bottoms of the boxes were made of wood.

In 1957, Ford began to make boxes entirely out of steel. The new steel boxes had smooth sides. They no longer had steps. They had more cargo room.

In the 1970s, stepsides became popular again. Pickup makers offered buyers stepsides as an **option** on some models.

An important part of the box is the **tailgate**. The tailgate is a door at the back of the box. When the tailgate is closed, cargo cannot slide out of the box.

Box Accessories

Pickup owners can buy special parts just for the box. Because cargo can scratch the inside

Stepside pickups have a small step in front of each rear wheel. Until the 1950s, all boxes were stepsides.

of the box, some owners add **box liners**. These large plastic boxes fit inside the pickup box. They protect the paint from scratches.

Pickup owners can also put **toppers** on the boxes. Toppers add walls and a roof to the box. The toppers protect the driver's cargo. Rain and snow cannot get in the box.

Some toppers are large enough to sleep in. These toppers are called campers. Some campers have small kitchens and beds.

The extended cab was introduced by Dodge in 1973.

The Cab

The driver and passengers sit in the cab of a pickup. In 1928, Ford introduced the first closed cab. The closed cab protected people from foul weather. Before the closed cab was added, the driver and passengers sat on an open seat, like a wagon's.

The first pickups had **running boards** on the cab. Running boards are like steps. They are attached beneath the doors on both sides.

They are designed to help the driver and passengers get into the cab.

Most new trucks do not come with running boards. They are an option, though, on some models. Running boards are a favorite feature for people who add custom parts to their pickups.

Most pickup cabs have one long seat. Only three people can ride in them.

In 1973, Dodge introduced the **extended cab**. It has two small seats behind the long front seat. People can use these seats. Some drivers use the extended cab's extra room to store gear they do not want to put in the box.

The Engine

The first pickups had small engines with four **cylinders**. Sometimes the four-cylinder engines did not give the truck as much power as the driver needed. In 1932, Ford introduced a pickup with a **V-8** engine. This engine has eight cylinders instead of four.

Most full-size pickup trucks today have powerful V-8 engines.

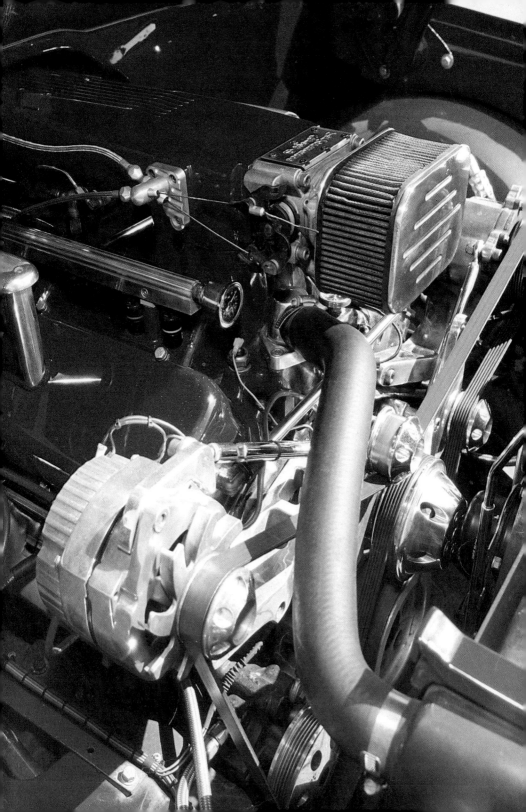

An eight-cylinder engine can spin the **drive shaft** faster than a four-cylinder engine. The drive shaft is a long rod under the truck. When the truck is in gear, the drive shaft spins and turns the truck's wheels.

The drive shafts on most pickups turn only the rear wheels. These pickups have **two-wheel drive**.

A V-8 engine gives the pickup more power. Today, most full-size pickups have eight-cylinder engines.

But eight-cylinder engines need a lot of gas. In the 1950s, some pickups were made with six-cylinder engines to save gas. Today, many smaller pickups have four-cylinder engines. These smaller trucks are not made for heavy work.

Smaller trucks are not made for heavy work. They usually have four-cylinder or six-cylinder engines.

Chapter 4

Pickups at Play

The first pickups were sturdier than cars. They could go places cars could not go. People realized they could have fun with pickups. They could drive through woods and water. They could drive up some mountains. Pickups became even more popular when **four-wheel** drive was invented.

Four-Wheel Drive

Pickups with four-wheel drive are called **4x4s**. In a 4x4, the drive shaft can turn either two wheels or four wheels. When all four wheels turn, the pickup has more power and **traction**.

Four-wheel drive pickups are perfect for off-road driving.

Car makers in the United States sell more pickups than cars.

If you want to know what two-wheel drive is like, try to climb a steep hill with just your feet. It can be difficult because you do not have much traction.

Then try to climb the hill on your hands and knees. It will be easier because you have more traction. Getting down on all fours is like having four-wheel drive.

Turning it On

Some 4x4s have a switch or button on the dashboard that turns on the four-wheel drive. Other 4x4s have a shift lever on the floor of the cab. When the shift lever is pushed into position, the drive shaft powers all four wheels.

On other 4x4s, the front wheels have keys on their **hubs**. When the keys are switched into position, the four-wheel drive is turned on. With this system, the driver must stop the truck and get out to turn on the four-wheel drive.

29

The First 4x4s

Four-wheel drive was invented for military vehicles. Army trucks often needed to get through deep mud. After World War II, many people bought the army's old vehicles.

They raced the trucks over sand dunes and through mud. With four-wheel drive, the old army trucks could go places even pickups could not.

Because the old army trucks were so popular, truck makers in the 1950s started making pickups with four-wheel drive.

The first four-wheel drive pickups were perfect for **off-road** driving. Since then, off-road racing has become a popular sport. Drivers today use their 4x4 pickups for hill-climbing and **mud-bogging**.

Monster Trucks

In 1974, a man named Bob Chandler bought a blue 4x4. Many people near Chandler's hometown of Hazelwood, Missouri, also owned 4x4s. When their 4x4s broke down, they asked

New pickups still have the same basic design as the first pickups.

Chandler to fix them. Chandler went into business fixing 4x4s.

To attract customers, Chandler **customized** his own 4x4. He parked it in front of his business. With the money he made repairing other people's 4x4s, Chandler bought new parts for his own truck. Those new parts included huge tires. As the truck got bigger, more customers came to Chandler's garage.

The Nickname

Chandler liked to race his truck. When he raced, he stepped heavily on the gas pedal. His friends called him Bigfoot.

Chandler painted his nickname on his blue 4x4. His pickup was unlike any other truck. People called it a monster truck.

Today, Chandler has 14 Bigfoot trucks. Except for the fact that they are all blue, each Bigfoot is different.

The tires range from five to 10 feet (1.5 to three meters) tall. Each truck weighs between six and eight tons (5.4 and 7.2 metric tons).

Monster truck tires can be 10 feet (three meters) tall.

They are expensive to build. Because the Bigfoot trucks are so big, they need engines five times more powerful than car engines.

To pay for the trucks, Chandler gets money from **sponsors**. He then paints the sponsors' names on his trucks.

Monsters Everywhere

Many people today build monster trucks. The owners travel to arenas and stadiums all over the world. The arenas and stadiums are filled with dirt, mud, and old cars. There, drivers race their monster trucks against each other.

Monster truck drivers have contests to see who can climb the steepest hills. They see who can drive through the deepest mud. They see who can crush the most old cars.

These events attract millions of fans. Some of the best trucks today are Goliath, King Krunch, Snake Bite, Grave Digger, Bear Foot, Extreme Overkill, and Nitemare.

Monster truck events attract millions of fans each year.

Hot Rod Trucks

Another way people have fun with their pickups is by customizing them. Customizing started because the first cars and trucks looked so much alike. People wanted their cars and pickups to look different than everybody else's.

So they made changes to reflect their tastes. Some owners painted their cars and trucks different colors. Others bought or made special equipment to make their cars and trucks faster. These customized cars and pickups were the first **hot rods**.

Hot rods are as popular as ever. Hot rodders like old pickups. They find them in fields and junkyards and buy them for very little money. Once the pickups are repaired and customized, they look brand new.

Some pickup owners fix and paint old trucks until they look brand new. These trucks are called hot rods.

Hot rod owners like to fix up old trucks they find in fields and junkyards. (Photo next page)

Chapter 5

Pickups for Everyone

Over the years, pickup makers have tried new designs. In 1957, Chevrolet introduced the El Camino. It was lower than a pickup. It looked like a car with a shallow box. Chevrolet built the El Camino for more than 20 years.

Some people use pickups as family vehicles. But in the 1970s, there was a gas shortage. In some places, people had to wait in long lines to buy gas. A lot of gas stations ran out of gas. Gas became expensive.

So Chevy built a small pickup that used less gas than a full-sized truck. It was called the

People buy pickups for both work and play.

The El Camino looked like a car with a shallow box.

Luv. Luv stood for light-utility vehicle. Although Chevy no longer makes the Luv, Japanese and U.S. car makers still build small pickups that use less gas.

Pickups are more popular than ever. People buy pickups for work, for play, and just to get around. In the United States, car makers sell more new pickups than new cars.

New trucks still have the same basic design as the first pickups. It is a sound design. It has lasted a long time. There is no doubt that the pickup is here to stay.

Pickups are used at the ocean to patrol the beaches.

Glossary

box—back part of a pickup used for hauling cargo

box liner—plastic box that fits inside a pickup's box and prevents the paint inside the steel box from being scratched

cab—the part of a pickup with doors and a roof over the driver and passengers

cargo—goods and supplies carried in a pickup's box

customizing—changing a vehicle according to the owner's needs and tastes

cylinders—can-shaped areas of an engine that hold the pistons where gas is ignited

drive shaft—long rod that connects the engine to the wheels

extended cab—pickup cab with two small seats behind the longer front seat

flatbed—truck with no box

4x4—truck with four-wheel drive

four-wheel drive—special feature that allows the engine to turn all four wheels, not just the two back wheels

hot rod—customized car or pickup
hub—the center of a wheel
light-duty truck—another name for a pickup
mud-bogging—racing four-wheel drive pickups through deep mud
off-road—sport in which four-wheel drive pickups are driven on unpaved roads
option—feature that a buyer can have added to a new pickup
running board—step beneath a pickup's door to help people in and out
sponsor—company that gives money in exchange for advertising
stepside—box with a small step in front of each rear wheel
tailgate—door at the rear of a pickup box
topper—protective covering placed over a pickup's box
traction—measure of how tires grip the ground
two-wheel drive—when the engine delivers power to only two of the truck's wheels
utility truck—old style of truck used only for work
V-8—an engine with eight cylinders

To Learn More

Donahue, A.K. *4x4s and Pickups.* Mankato, Minn.: Capstone Press, 1991.

Dorin, Patrick C. *Yesterday's Trucks.* Minneapolis: Lerner Publications Company, 1982.

Fetherston, David A. *Heroes of Hot Rodding.* Osceola, Wis.: Motorbooks International, 1992.

Johnston, Scott D. *Monster Truck Racing.* Mankato, Minn.: Capstone Press, 1994.

Pernu, Dennis. *Hot Rods.* Mankato, Minn.: Capstone Press, 1995.

You can read articles about pickups in the following magazines: *Truckin', Trucks, Hot Rod,* and *Petersen's 4 Wheel & Off-Road.*

Useful Addresses

American Truck Historical Society
201 Office Park Drive
Birmingham, AL 35223

Monster Truck Racing Association
6311 Lindbergh
Hazelwood, MO 63042

National Hot Rod Association (NHRA)
2035 Financial Way
Glendora, CA 91740

Historical Automobile Society of Canada
14 Elizabeth Street
Guelph, ON N1E 2X2
Canada

Index